Outdoor Spaces
In The Southwest

Damon Lang

with Darlene Claire Preussner

Illustrations by Edgar Herrera
Photography by Damon Lang, unless otherwise noted
Designs and Installations by Damon Lang and Green Planet Landscaping

4880 Lower Valley Road, Atglen, Pa 19310

Schiffer Books are available at special discounts for bulk purchases for sales promotions or premiums. Special editions, including personalized covers, corporate imprints, and excerpts can be created in large quantities for special needs. For more information contact the publisher:

Published by Schiffer Publishing Ltd.
4880 Lower Valley Road
Atglen, PA 19310
Phone: 610-593-1777; Fax: 610-593-2002
E-mail: Info@schifferbooks.com

For the largest selection of fine reference books on this and related subjects, please visit our web site at
www.schifferbooks.com
We are always looking for people to write books on new and related subjects. If you have an idea for a book please contact us at the above address.

This book may be purchased from the publisher.
Include $5.00 for shipping.
Please try your bookstore first.
You may write for a free catalog.

In Europe, Schiffer books are distributed by
Bushwood Books
6 Marksbury Ave.
Kew Gardens
Surrey TW9 4JF England
Phone: 44 (0) 20 8392-8585; Fax: 44 (0) 20 8392-9876
E-mail: info@bushwoodbooks.co.uk
Website: www.bushwoodbooks.co.uk
Free postage in the U.K., Europe; air mail at cost.

Designed by RoS
Type set in Eras Bk BT/Dutch 809 BT

ISBN: 978-0-7643-3214-2
Printed in China

Contents

"Victory" 3/14/94
is certain if we have
the courage to believe and
the strength to run our
own race.

Acknowledgements

Where do I start? There are so many people to thank both professionally and personally. Putting this book together has been an amazing journey and a labor of love. Thinking back on the number of books I have purchased over the years, their importance and inspiration, it is my sincere hope that this book will inspire others.

I want to begin by thanking Schiffer Publishing for giving me the opportunity to write this book. Thank you, Tina Skinner, for finding my website and offering me the chance of a lifetime. Thank you, Darlene Claire Preussner, for helping me transform my thoughts and words into something tangible. You did such a great job! I know how trying it was to juggle our demanding schedule at GPL with the needs of this book. To Kim Mills, Thank you for all the years of hard work, loyalty and dedication. Without you, so many of my ideas and dreams would have never become a reality. It has been such a rewarding journey together and something I will never forget….Great Job, Princess! To my GPL team, past and present, thank you for bringing all my crazy ideas to fruition. Hopefully, you are as proud of this book as I am. To Pamela Quigley, thank you for helping my designs come to life with your plant knowledge. To my generous clients that allowed me to make their dreams a reality, thank you for your loyalty and most of all, trust in me and GPL.

And on a personal note, there are my wonderful and supportive parents to thank for teaching me how important it is to do the right thing and instilling in me my work ethic and morals. Mom, thanks for the words of wisdom and insight when I needed them. Dad, thanks for keeping an eye on GPL with me and your advice over the years. You are my balance wheel! I'm so proud to have you as parents. Since the incep-

tion of GPL, you both have been a great source of love and support. I don't think I express this enough in everyday life – Thank You and I Love You! To my brothers who have brought me laughter and support – Love you guys. My sister in laws Brenda and Liz, thanks for the support. (See Liz, I can write a book – I know it's not quite a pop-up book – but I'm working on that one next. See Damon Dig!) To Sophie and Scotty, my niece and nephew, welcome to the family. I am so glad to have the two of you in my life.

To Karen, thank you for teaching me Ansara yoga and being a part of my life. You have taught me the importance of balancing body and mind and that life is about balance. I am inspired by you and yoga every day. Love you!

To Gary, my best friend. For being there through thick and thin, giving me the love and support that will last a lifetime. For lifting my spirits when they were down. For listening as I rambled about my projects and the company. For the inspiration you bring to my life. Thank You.

To my other best friend, Max, my Labrador Retriever. Thank you for holding it in when I arrived home late and for testing new dog friendly products. For all the unconditional love you give me and for always being happy to see me no matter what kind of day I've faced or my mood.

To my other friends and family that are important to me not mentioned above. What is life without family and friends?

And finally, to Howard Jenkins, thanks for giving me the opportunity to start my career as a landscape designer. Your guidance and wisdom is something I will never forget. I hope I can pass along the torch to future designers. I will always remember that small note you gave me back in 1994……..

Preface

My intention with writing this book is to inspire new ideas and share my thoughts on building a functional design. I want to keep the technical aspect to a minimum; instead, my aim is towards inspiration, practical ideas, and design solutions. Since the majority of the projects take place in the desert, I want to assist those in similar climates. Our material selection is limited in the arid region. I have provided images of products and materials I use every day.

Damon Lang with clients in his GPL office. Photography by Darlene Claire.

Low levels at Lake Mead. Photos courtesy of the Southern Nevada Water Authority.

On the other hand, I try to be conscious of global warming and other environmental issues. Since the start of my career, great strides have been taken towards conserving natural resources. Whenever possible, I guide clients to incorporate green products and drought-tolerant xeriscape. Not only is appropriate plant selection important, but also finding new materials and installation techniques. Seeing first hand the water level of our largest manmade lake, Lake Mead, drop 75 feet and there is no denying that we all need to do what we can to improve the situation. Forget arguing whether it's cycles or not. What we do today will affect what happens tomorrow. I am active in the Southern Nevada Water Authority conservation programs, test new products that are eco-friendly, and, whenever possible, I incorporate recycled materials.

Simple principles and a combination of instinct and imagination are what help me create a great project.

A great design space can nurture personal well being by balancing inner and outer peace. A garden exposes us to fresh air, water, plants, and sunshine — all vital to human existence. Since we probably work more hours than our parents did, it is even more important that we enjoy our quality time. Typically, we work 9-to-5 days, and by the time we get home there is little or no sunlight left to enjoy the outdoors. Illuminating outdoor kitchens and outdoor rooms can make a world of difference. Even more important are design elements, such as fireplaces and firepits to extend time spent outside.

A creative garden can introduce us to things we never had the opportunity to do or see.

Sunken rose garden.

First, A Yard is Born

Designing your outdoor living space may seem like a daunting task. There are endless possibilities for how to use the area. Add to it the infinite selection and combination of materials available for installation and it becomes almost overwhelming to even consider. But whether or not you have had experience in a related field, preparation is truly the key to success. Creating a personal paradise that reflects the style, taste and individuality of the homeowner brings not only a sense of satisfaction, but also improves the quality of life and the value of the home. It is the only home improvement that appreciates both aesthetically and financially over time.

First things first! Decide how the area is to be used and by whom. Set realistic goals for what you want to achieve from the project. Lifestyle is an important consideration. Is what you want and need:
– Privacy, seclusion and a place to escape for a while
– Relaxing under a shade tree to read a book or watch the sunset
– Entertaining with your flair for cooking and dining alfresco
– Quality time with the family and a safe environment for the children and pets
– A picturesque setting you can appreciate through an interior window
– All of the above

The majority of us believe we know ourselves. At the very least, we know what we like and what we dislike. Determining your individual style and taste is a process of information gathering and portfolio building. As you thumb through magazines or pictures, save examples of anything that pleases and make a notation of why you find it appealing. Home improvement stores are a goldmine for ideas. Collect samples of paint colors, tile pieces, stone or pavers, even varying textures. A trend or pattern should emerge. During this process, try not to be inhibited by budget or other mitigating factors. Consider these steps:
– Determine functional goal
– Identify aesthetic goal
– Develop a well reasoned plan
– Implement the plan in an orderly fashion
– Execute design plan

The mosaic inlet above and the water sheers on either side balance the unusual height of the stone chimney.

An artificial turf putting green.

Above left:
Raised dining area.

Above right:
This contemporary water feature pays tribute to the moon and stars. Photography by Beth Mehocic

Left:
Dining area near the outdoor kitchen.

Right:
A scupper juts out from a mosaic glass tiled wall.

Nestled in the corner of the yard is an exposed aggregate patio bordered with stamped concrete.

A garage door is transformed into a view into a Tuscan villa.

An aluminum lattice patio cover shades the spa.

Now that the goals are set and a style is being nurtured comes time for the site assessment. This requires accurate measurements and clear photographs. A two dimensional overhead plan will result from measuring the home's exterior walls, the property walls, the distances between each and architectural features contained in the house. Windows, doors, steps, patios and columns all must be noted with the coordinating dimensions including height. Existing features within the property need identification, even if your intension is to have it removed. Realize the elements of the existing landscape you intend to keep and if it makes sense to reposition them. Locate and indicate utility hook ups for gas, electric and water accessibility. Contact your local building department or home owners association for codes and restrictions that apply.

Photograph the area from all sides and angles. Pay particular attention to focal opportunities from inside the residence out windows and upon entering through the front door. Take pictures at regular intervals to track the sun's exposure, keeping in mind the slight variation from season to season. Having images of the property allows for immediate reference whether on site or not. Being able to compare before and after is greatly rewarding.

Have the necessary tools to measure and photograph before starting your plan.

At this point you may be asking yourself, "Why am I going to all this trouble? Is a design really necessary?" Having a landscape plan saves both time and money. Think of the design as a roadmap that will take you in the direction you want to go and get you there the best way possible. If you find that the direction you're heading leads to a dead end, it is much easier to start over on paper. On occasion, what works on the plan does not work in actuality. Spray paint the design on the ground as accurately as possible and take a test drive. Live and walk around the space for several days to get an idea of how or if it functions the way you anticipated. Organizing your thoughts not only determines the budget for the overall project, it allows for the opportunity to implement the concept in stages. Contractors provide quotes more accurately from a plan and each bid is comparative to the other.

View from inside living room.

A stained concrete sun sets in the rake garden.

Hardscape defines the space and must be positioned in the plan first. This is when you need to know your furniture selection. What?! That's correct. Furniture is always placed in an activity area and of some importance. Put the spacial needs in an abstract form such as a bubble, whereas the shape can easily be manipulated leaving the size requirements the same. Each gathering area requiring furniture placement needs a transitional zone connecting them together. This can be noted on your plan with a symbol such as an arrow to describe traffic flows or patterns.

Tropical courtyard sitting area.

Ying and yang depicted in acid stained concrete.

Above:
Bright comfortable funiture completes this elevated poolside lounging area.

Left:
Roman columns add elegance to the lounging area.

Tuscan Treasure

Spacious, yet charming, this opulent Tuscan home blends traditional with technical, fanciful with refined seamlessly. The expansive entryway leading to the house is laid with concrete pavers, much like cobblestone, past grape vines supported on a trellis. Like the region that inspired the architecture, wining and dining are an essential part of everyday lifestyle. The property displays this culture in true eloquence and flair. Anchoring and focal to the rear of the property is a magnificent stone fireplace complete with an LCD outdoor television. Balancing the yard is a complete outdoor kitchen with a granite countertop, seating guests with the best possible view of the liquid light show.

Around the side of the house is a hidden treasure. A dramatic fire and water feature adorned with black iridescent tile which mirrors the visual effect and multiplies its impact. A perfect mix of elegant and elaborate, indoors and out, shows truly the best that life has to offer.

Artist conception of design.

Centerpiece in the expansive backyard, the warm glow from this majestic stone and brick veneer fireplace keeps guests socializing long after dark.

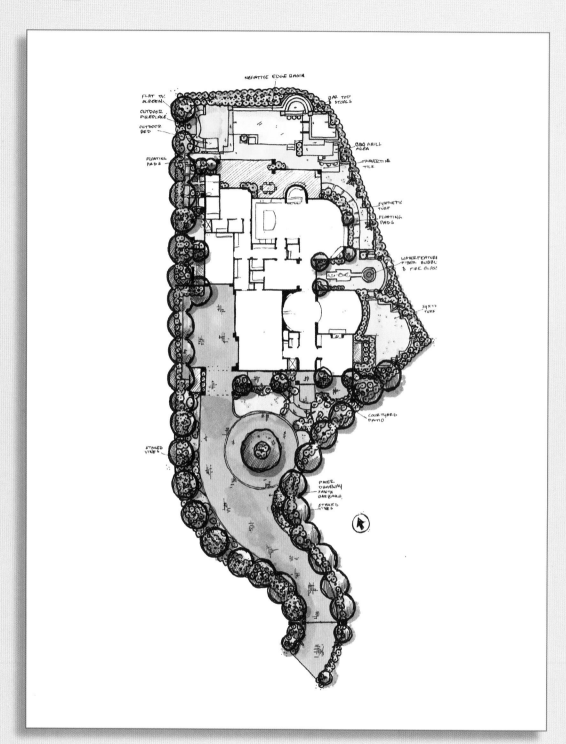

Overhead rendering of the property.

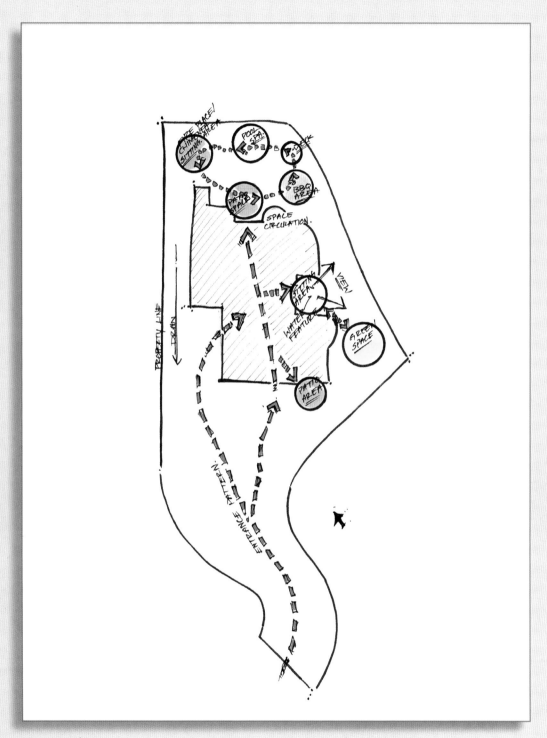

Concept plan.

Before images.

This Tuscan villa appears as if transplanted from an Italian countryside.

The rear balcony overlooks a low profile fire pot.

Synthetic turf encircles the Roman style columns in the courtyard.

Wrought iron grapes adorn the entry gate and set the tone for what awaits.

Vineyards line the driveway leading to the home.

Guests are awarded a panoramic view of the Las Vegas strip at the eating countertop.

A floating pad walkway leads to hidden visual treasures.

The chef is given a glorious view of the golf course.

A granite countertop and stone veneer add elegance to the kitchen.

Runnels spill water into the pool from the wet deck.

A bronze scupper pours water from the center of a mosiac travertine tile wall.

The ever changing light display is in true Las Vegas style.

Cushions and
pillows customize
the outdoor bed.

An artificial log set
brings an indoor
element outside.

Dining room guests are treated with a
view of the fire and water feature.

Seated at the custom bench, clean lines
draw the eye to the interior dining room.

Bubblers erupt

around the

floating pads.

Fiber optic
bubblers
enhance the
view from the
interior dining
area.

The iridescent tile gives off a prism of hues, ever changing throughout the day.

Blending colored fire glass achieved a perfect match to the tile.

A flaming wok bowl seems to float on top of the water.

Outdoor lighting casts dramatic shadows and distinct outlines.

Water hugs the iridescent glass tile.

An erupting bubbler can be seen through the runnel.

The fire is
manifested
in the
sunset.

Top left:
Laminars spring colorful arcs across the water.

Middle left:
An ever changing color wheel adds drama to the runnel and spa bubblers.

Bottom left:
The wet deck becomes a spectacular light display after dark.

At night the wet
deck is transformed
into an incredible
focal point.

Nature provides moonlit mountain views from the spa.

PROJECT KEY

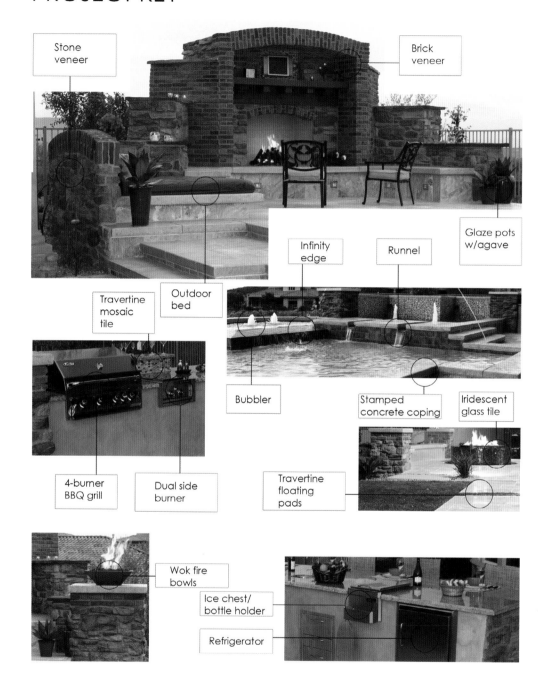

Stone veneer

Brick veneer

Infinity edge

Runnel

Glaze pots w/agave

Travertine mosaic tile

Outdoor bed

Bubbler

Stamped concrete coping

Iridescent glass tile

4-burner BBQ grill

Dual side burner

Travertine floating pads

Wok fire bowls

Ice chest/ bottle holder

Refrigerator

PROJECT KEY

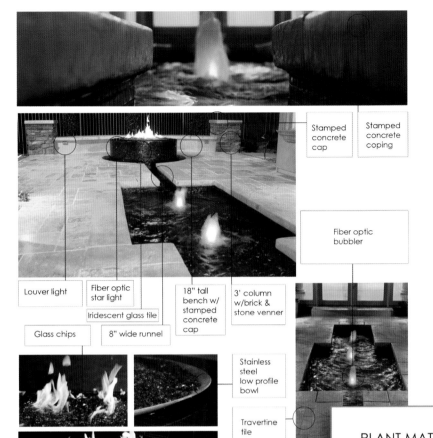

Stamped concrete cap

Stamped concrete coping

Fiber optic bubbler

Louver light

Fiber optic star light

Iridescent glass tile

18" tall bench w/ stamped concrete cap

3' column w/brick & stone venner

Glass chips

8" wide runnel

Stainless steel low profile bowl

Travertine tile

Weir

PLANT MATERIALS

1. Carolina Cherry Laurel Tree
2. Little Gem Magnolia
3. Lily Turf
4. Indian Hawthorn
5. Red Flame Grape Vines
6. Swan Hill Olive Tree
7. Texas Privet
8. Multi-trunk African Sumac

Poker Paradise

When a professional poker player contacts you to design and install a complete outdoor environment, you pose the same question, "What is your goal for this property?" When the response is, "To kick everyone's butt in the Country Club!", you have come face to face with a true gambler and Las Vegas local…bold, fun loving, entertaining and always playing to win. The backyard design had to capture that spirit.

Saying the site was ideal would be bluffing. The challenge was to accommodate the poker player's "all or nothing – the sky's the limit" attitude into the relatively small, irregular pie shaped lot. Raised 18" off the ground, the pool's infinity edge created a 56' swim lane by day and transformed into a mirror image of the Las Vegas Strip by night. Mini, laser lit, Bellagio Hotel style water features arch over a poker chip set in the wet deck floor plaster while a floating table awaits a waterproof deck of cards nearby.

To entertain like a poker player, you have to raise the stakes (or steaks) in an outdoor kitchen. The "U" arrangement satisfies both the captured cook and the guests seated directly opposite. What do you need to keep warm on cool Sin City nights? A firepit. This card shark holds a pair! One near the outdoor kitchen for comfort while dining alfresco. The second larger firepit is across the pool and surrounded by bed/bench style seating.

The final touch is an 1100 square foot putting green complete with rolling greens, sand traps and nine holes. A true stroke of genius.

Artist conception of design.

A blazing
firepit
warms
diners
at the
outdoor
kitchen.

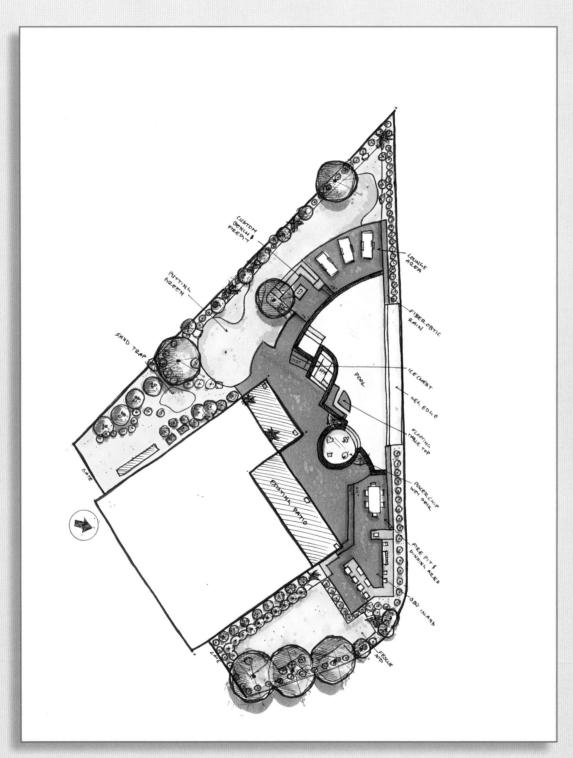

Overhead rendering of the property.

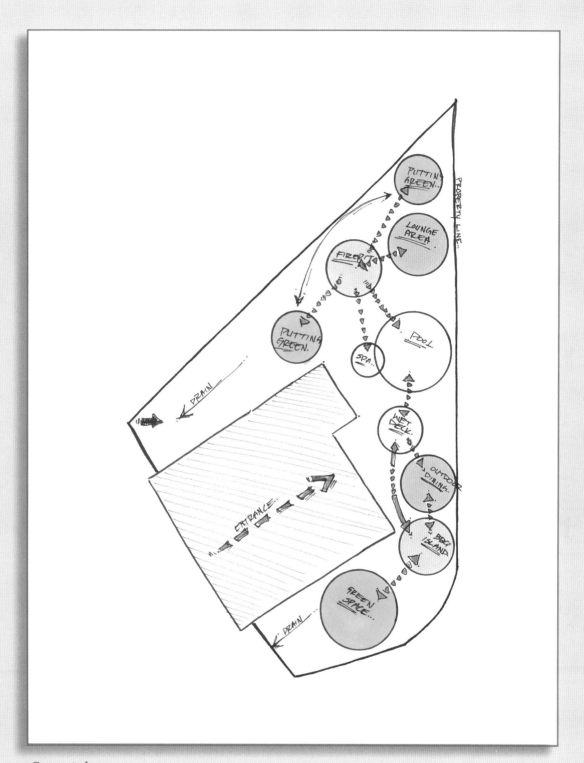

Concept plan.

A 56-foot swim lane took advantage of the irregular pie shaped lot.

Comfortable bed/bench style seating surrounds the second firepit.

Mosaic glass tile accents the reverse infinity edge of the spa.

Emerging
swimmers are
warmed by the
lounging area
firepit.

This 1100 square foot putting green is complete with rolling hills, nine holes and sand traps.

Mosaic glass tile accents the backdrop of the fiber optic rain descent.

The reverse infinity edge on the spa creates a dramatic water effect visible through the master bedroom window.

An ice chest set into the concrete is within arm's reach of the pool and spa.

An eating countertop affords guests the best view of the Las Vegas strip.

Fiber optic laminars arch over the larger than life betting token set in the pool's wet deck.

A poker chip emblem was set in the pool's wet deck.

The covered patio provides much needed shade for the master bedroom.

Lines and curves lead the eye to design elements.

The V-shaped kitchen allows the cook easy access to all the amenities.

Poker Paradise

A floating table caters to swim up guests.

A professional grade blender and kegerator are mounted on the bora bora granite countertop.

Illuminated grill knobs

Stone veneer and a stamped concrete cap finish this firepit.

Overstuffed weatherproof pillows and cushions adorn the bed/bench seating enclosing the firepit to keep guests comfy and toasty.

A firepit keeps guests warm while dining after sunset.

PROJECT KEY

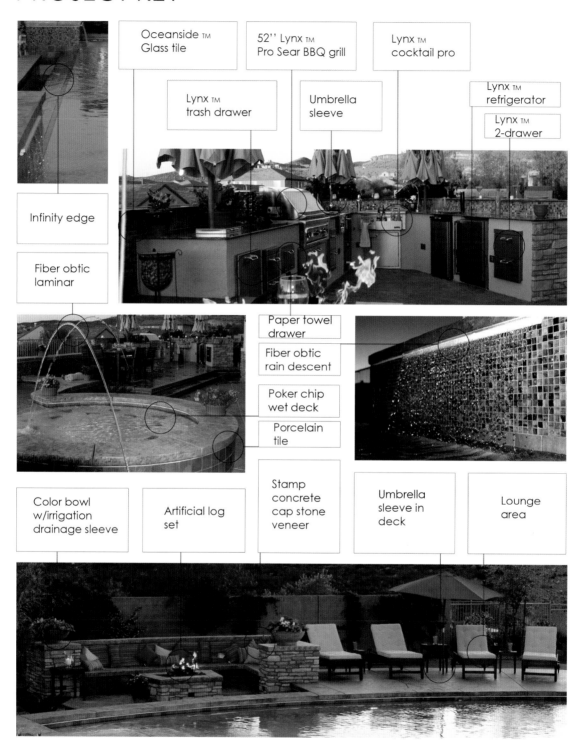

Oceanside ™ Glass tile

52'' Lynx ™ Pro Sear BBQ grill

Lynx ™ cocktail pro

Lynx ™ trash drawer

Umbrella sleeve

Lynx ™ refrigerator

Lynx ™ 2-drawer

Infinity edge

Fiber obtic laminar

Paper towel drawer

Fiber obtic rain descent

Poker chip wet deck

Porcelain tile

Color bowl w/irrigation drainage sleeve

Artificial log set

Stamp concrete cap stone veneer

Umbrella sleeve in deck

Lounge area

PLANT MATERIALS

1. Dwarf Lime & Lemon Tree
2. Japanese Blueberry
3. Color bowl/ Petunia
4. Lily Turf/Dwarf Bottle Brush
5. Sago Palm

Vintage Vegas

Reminiscent of a Tuscan villa, this backyard landscape is truly intoxicating. Avid wine enthusiasts with a passion for cooking and entertaining, the homeowners inspired the bistro seating area entwined with Chardonnay and Cabernet Sauvignon grape vines. A flagstone path meanders through a miniature orchard of lemon, lime, orange and grapefruit trees to the dining center. Beyond the outdoor kitchen, the walkway transitions to slate tile flooring an exterior living room. Wisteria vines embrace the lattice awning adding a sense of privacy and enclosure to the majestic stone fireplace. Putting and chipping greens rest at the base of a 25' berm, transformed into a functional focal point with a free flowing stream and cascading waterfall system. Flagstone steps and bridges criss cross a path to the summit to see the best feature the property has to offer, a stunning view of the entire Las Vegas Valley.

Artist conception of the design.

Designed to appear as an extension of the home, the fireplace is in plain view as visitors enter through the front door.

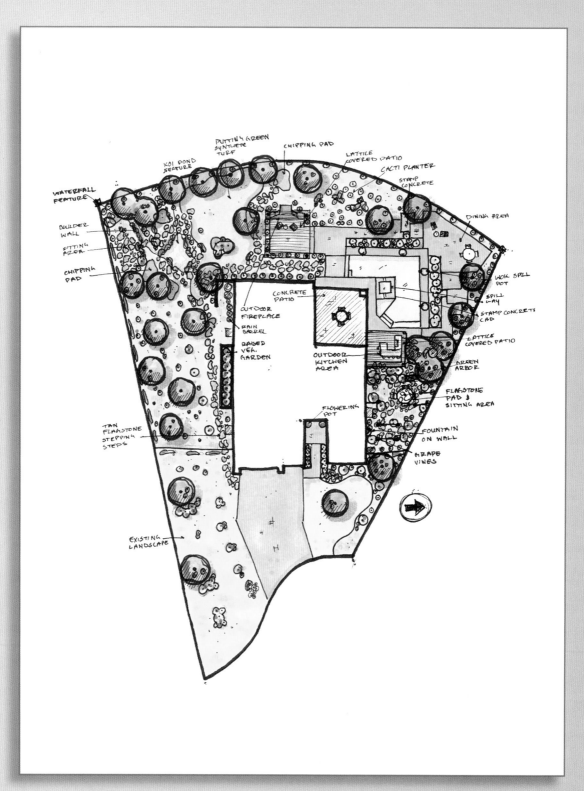

Overhead rendering of the property.

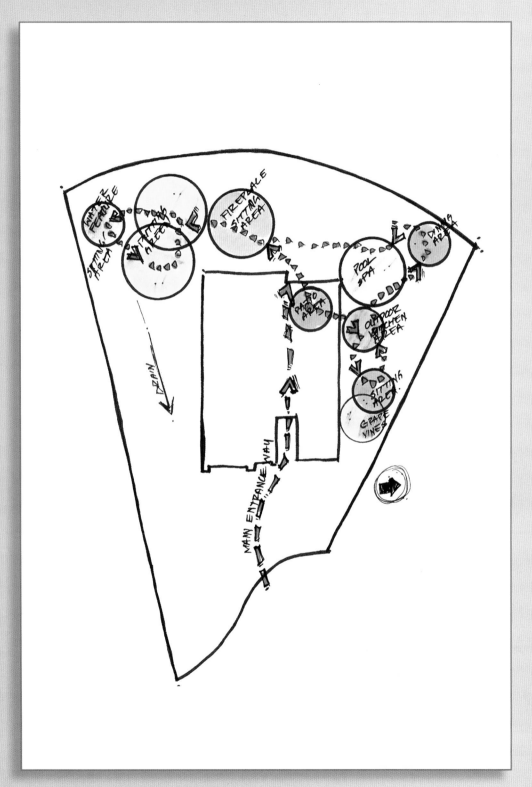

Concept plan.

Before images.

Artificial turf enables a perfectly groomed putting green year round.

Water conserving and environmentally responsible xeriscape was used in landscaping the yard.

This covered seating area enjoys the sights and sounds of the waterfall.

A large putting green with multiple chipping pads challenges the most avid golfer.

Blending boulders and chunky 2" to 4" rock mimics Mother Earth.

A planter island cut out of the turf is anchored by Sago palms.

Flagstone steps
cut a safe path to
the summit.

Brilliant pink blossoms stand in stark contrast to the desert vegetation.

A 25 foot slope was transformed into a stream and waterfall system which spills into a koi pond at the base.

Flagstone paths meander around the property.

Wisteria vines embrace the
pergola providing shade, color
and fragrance. Photography by
Eryn Ence.

The bistro
seating area is
entwined with
Chardonnay
and Cabernet
Sauvignon grape
vines.

A wok bowl spills water into the pool.

A kegerator guarantees cold draft on tap. Photography by Eryn Ence.

A slate walkway connects the different vignettes in the yard.

A U-shaped outdoor kitchen keeps the captured cook socializing. Photography by Eryn Ence.

A stunning view of
the Las Vegas valley
await those who
reach the top.

The most dramatic lighting is often provided by Mother Nature, her mood changing in mere moments. Photography by Eryn Ence.

Dramatic lighting can set the mood for late night gatherings.

Rope lighting adds the perfect ambiance for relaxing after dusk.

An elevated patio offers a magnificent view of the awesome sunsets. **Photography by Eryn Ence.**

Outdoor lighting enables extended hours of enjoyment.

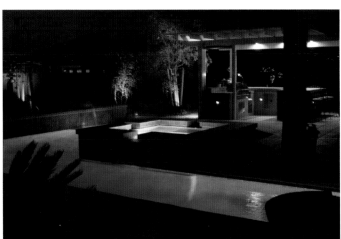

Water spills three ways from the spa into the pool.
Photography by Eryn Ence.

PROJECT KEY

Tulip pathlight

Aluminum lattice patio cover

Grape vine tile mosaic niche

Flagstone

Apache brown boulder

Artificial Putting green

Stone veneer

Quartzite tile floor

Colored concrete wok spill bowl

Stacked flagstone steps

Spray deck

Grand Turbo ™ grill w/side burner

Storage drawer

Kegerator

Trash drawer

Porcelain tile & stone veneer

Ornamental fountain w/Boston Ivy

PLANT MATERIALS

1. Red Flame Grapes
2. Multi-trunk African Sumac
3. Tangerine Beauty Cross Fire Vine
4. Yellow Barrel/Saguaro
5. Dwarf Bottlebrush
6. Purple Pad Cactus

Grace in a Small Space

Dominated by hardscape, the backyard of this vacation home is ready and waiting for guests to pamper. The small area appears as spacious and elegant as the home by utilizing multiple elevations and separate entertaining areas. The focal point upon entering the front door and centerpiece to the backyard is the water feature, which divides the fire pit and dining sections. An extension to the interior counterpart, the outdoor kitchen seats guests at a wrap around countertop. Situated in the uppermost corner of the property, an elevated fire pit with built in bench style seating hosts the best vantage point to overlook the neon sea in the valley below.

Artist conception of the design.

Centerpiece and focal point to the yard is this magnificent water feature.

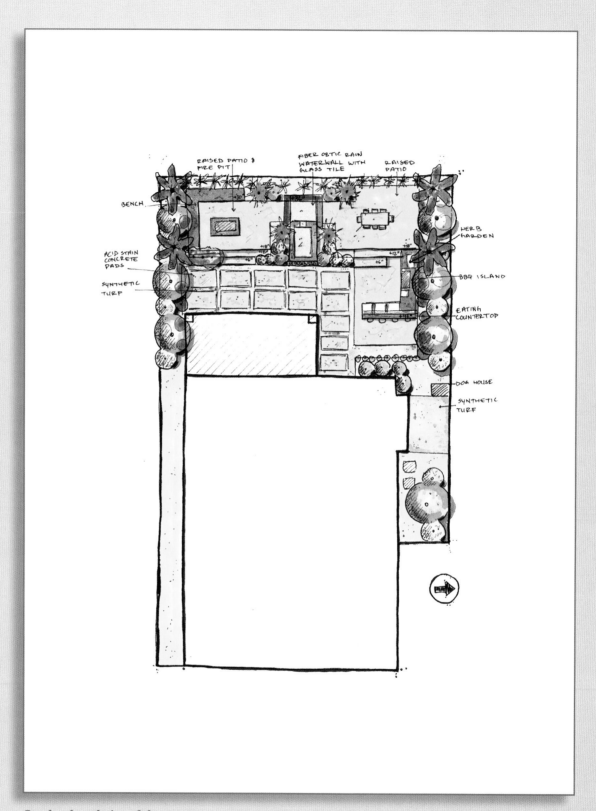

RAISED PATIO &
FIRE PIT

FIBER OPTIC RAIN
WATERWALL WITH
GLASS TILE

RAISED
PATIO

BENCH

HERB
GARDEN

ACID STAIN
CONCRETE
PADS

BBQ ISLAND

SYNTHETIC
TURF

EATING
COUNTERTOP

DOG HOUSE

SYNTHETIC
TURF

Overhead rendering of the property.

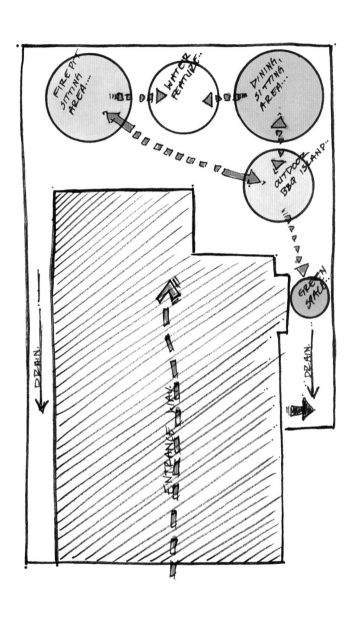

Concept plan.

Before images.

One side of the property hosts the outdoor kitchen and dining area.

Synthetic turf separates concrete, stained and scored to match the home's interior tile.

Photography by Steven Levey.

The outdoor kitchen matches the architectural style and materials of the house. Photography by Steven Levey.

Even the family pet was given consideration in the landscape design. Photography by Steven Levey.

The water feature can be viewed as guests arrive through the front door. Photography by Steven Levey.

The mosiac glass tile can be seen through the fiber optic rain descent. Photography by Steven Levey.

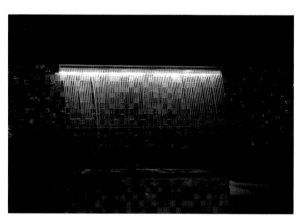

Strands of water appear to hang from the fiber optic rain descent. Photography by Steven Levey.

Step lighting assures guests reach the upper seating area safely. Photography by Steven Levey.

Bench style seating surrounds an elevated firepit on the other side.

Photography by Steven Levey.

A tranquil atmosphere is generated with outdoor lighting.
Photography by Steven Levey.

The state of the art outdoor kitchen is complete with an eating countertop and planter box herb garden.
Photography by Steven Levey.

A sink, ice chest, bottle opener, towel holder and bottle rack are all contained in the refreshment center.
Photography by Steven Levey.

PROJECT KEY

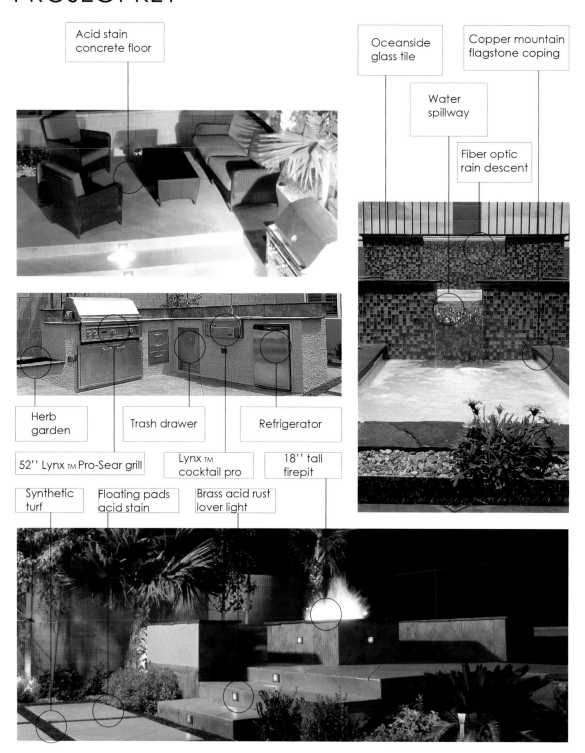

Acid stain concrete floor

Oceanside glass tile

Copper mountain flagstone coping

Water spillway

Fiber optic rain descent

Herb garden

Trash drawer

Refrigerator

52'' Lynx TM Pro-Sear grill

Lynx TM cocktail pro

18'' tall firepit

Synthetic turf

Floating pads acid stain

Brass acid rust lover light

PLANT MATERIALS

1. Gardenia
2. Sago Palm
3. Mexican Fan Palm
4. Winter Gem Boxwood
5. Gazania
6. Bottle Tree

Amber Glass with Class

Clean, straight lines dominate this backyard landscape to create a modern sophisticated feel. Masterfully blending cultured stone, glass tile and acid stained concrete gives the hardscape an elegant appearance. Cleverly masked within the plant material that softens the perimeter of the property are fun and fanciful pieces of garden art, a silent prelude to the nighttime transformation of the yard. A kaleidoscope of color and dancing water magically appear as the sun sets, like children coming out to play. Full of whimsy and delight, it touches the kindred spirit in all of us.

Artist conception of the design.

A metal
sculpture sits
majestically
atop her fluid
throne.

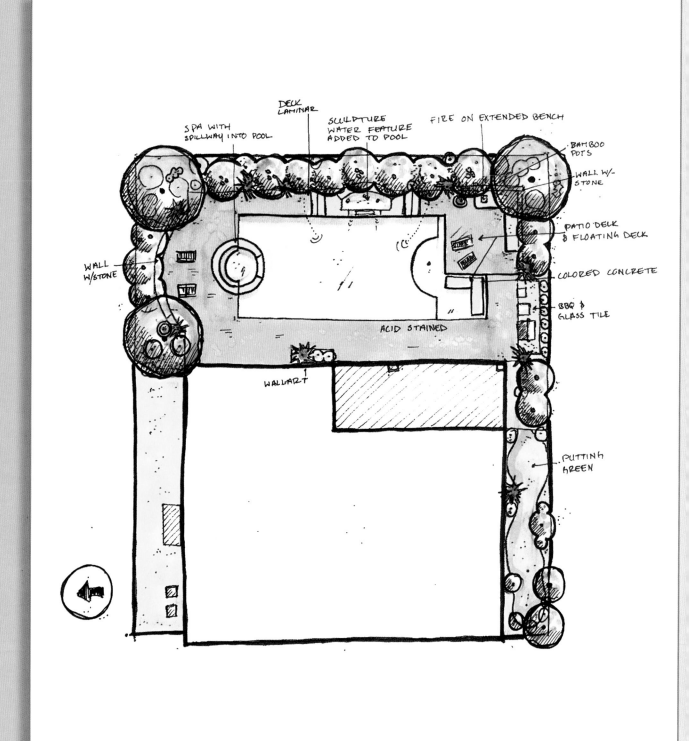

DECK
LAMINAR

SPA WITH
SPILLWAY INTO POOL

SCULPTURE
WATER FEATURE
ADDED TO POOL

FIRE ON EXTENDED BENCH

BAMBOO
POTS

WALL W/-
STONE

WALL
W/STONE

PATIO DECK
& FLOATING DECK

COLORED CONCRETE

BBQ &
GLASS TILE

ACID STAINED

WALL ART

PUTTING
GREEN

Overhead rendering of the property.

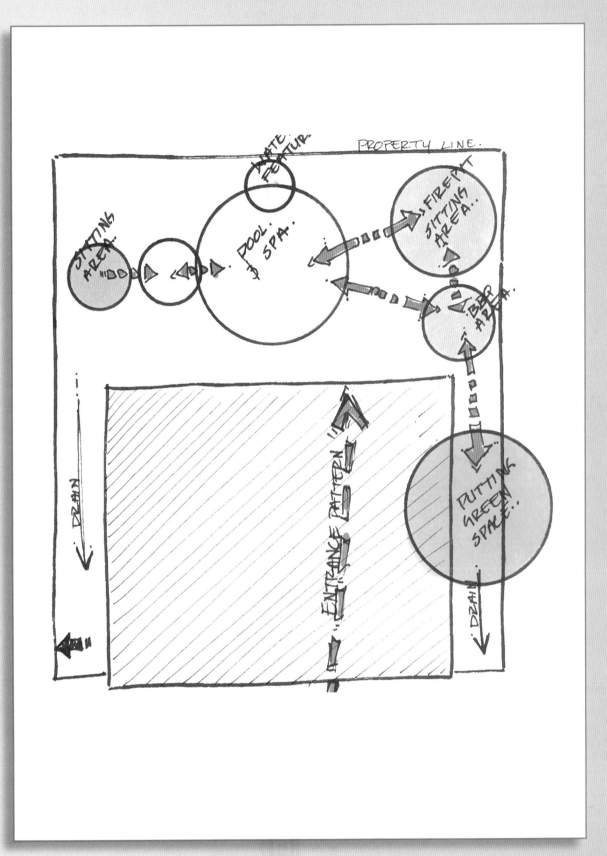

Concept plan.

Before images.

The stone veneer wall adds dimension and interest to the glass tiled spa.

The floating pad is evident in contrast to the acid stained concrete.

Playful garden art peeks out from behind the vegetation.

**Relax in the spa
and enjoy the
"eye candy"
around the yard.**

An artificial putting green is tucked behind the
house for private practice.

Capped with
concrete, the stone
columns and outdoor
kitchen are softened
with plant material.

The colored concrete and glass tile found throughout the yard is repeated in the outdoor kitchen.

Water spilling gently over the tile adds a touch of class.

A stone wall behind the firepit captures the warmth and glow of the flame.

Colored glass chips reflect the flickering light.

Hidden in the planter, the shooting fiber optic deck laminar is a pleasant surprise.

A chromatic display, dancing water and acoustic effects generate a festive atmosphere.

Bamboo
shoots in
a stainless
steel planter
add vertical
dimension.

A 24" raised multi-faceted water feature draws attention throughout the yard.

The floating pad fits like a puzzle piece in the pool coping.

PROJECT KEY

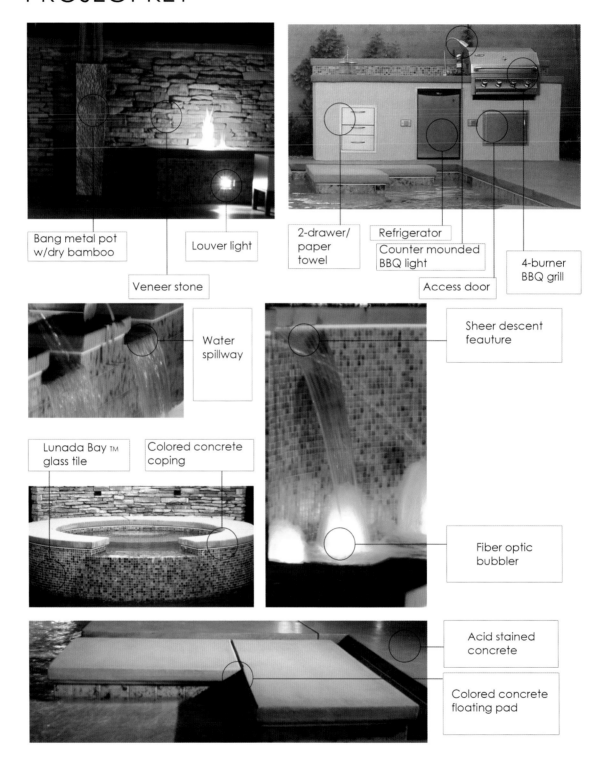

Bang metal pot w/dry bamboo

Louver light

Veneer stone

2-drawer/ paper towel

Refrigerator

Counter mounded BBQ light

Access door

4-burner BBQ grill

Water spillway

Sheer descent feauture

Lunada Bay ™ glass tile

Colored concrete coping

Fiber optic bubbler

Acid stained concrete

Colored concrete floating pad

PLANT MATERIALS

1. Dwarf Mock Orange
2. Sago Palm
3. Carolina Cherry
4. Multi-trunk African Sumac
5. Red-tip Photinia
6. Golden Eounymus

And then, there's Zen

The front yard landscape works in concert with the strong architectural elements of this modern contemporary home by adding a Zen like feel and drought tolerant Xeriscape. The home's clean perpendicular lines of mostly metal and concrete are softened with warm subtle shades of blue, green and grey. Simplistic in nature and modern in theme, the complete front yard landscape follows the striking angles, strong straight lines, varied textures and bold colors of the home. As you approach the entrance, a calm transcendental feeling envelopes the visitor, precipitating the warm reception inside.

Artist conception of the design.

A Zen-like feel
in the front
yard creates an
aura of good
karma.

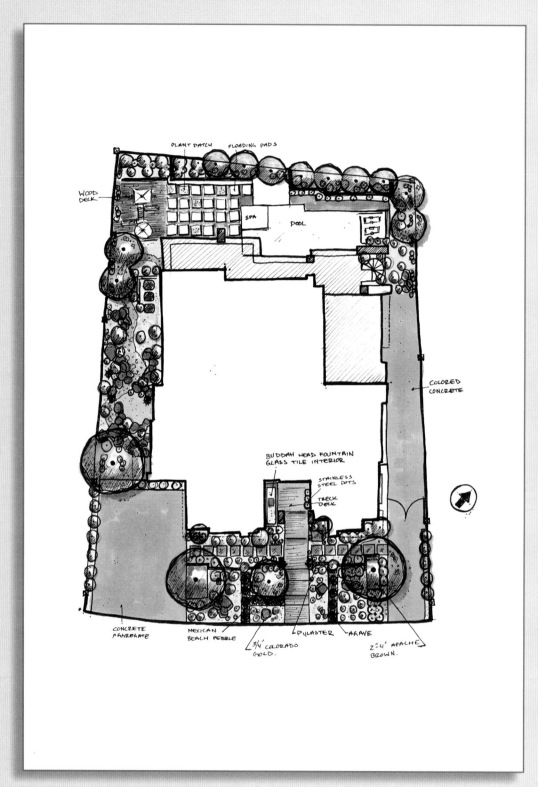

PLANT PATCH   FLOADING PADS

WOOD
DECK

SPA

POOL

COLORED
CONCRETE

BUDDAH HEAD FOUNTAIN
GLASS TILE INTERIOR

STAINLESS
STEEL POTS

TRECK
DECK

CONCRETE
PHAREGATE

MEXICAN
BEACH PEBBLE

PULASTER   AGAVE

3/4" COLORADO
GOLD.

2"-4" APACHE
BROWN.

Overhead rendering of the property.

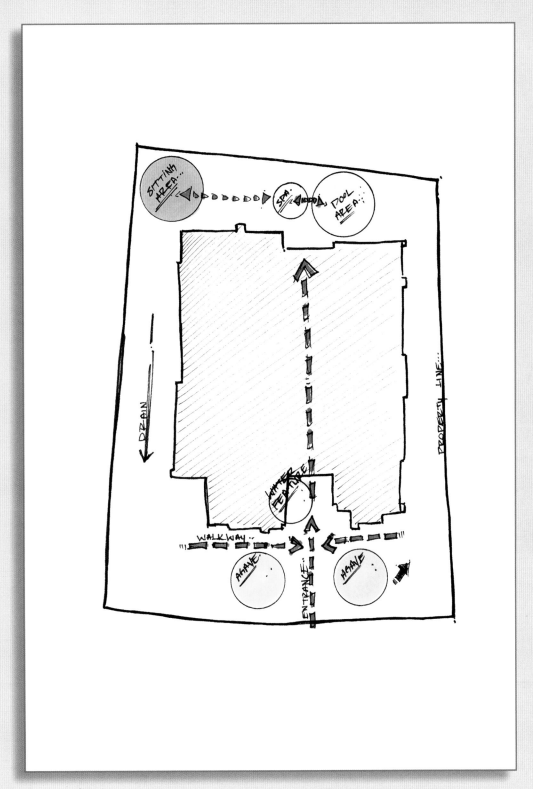

Concept plan.

Before images

Weeping yucca
adds contrast
in both texture
and color.

A series of offset vertical
concrete panels separate
the plantings creating a
courtyard feel.

Heavenly bamboo, mondo grass and yew pines transplant an air of Eastern influence.

Stainless steel pots magnify the details on the front doors.

Smiling to greet
visitors is a
massive Buddha
head fountain
gazing over
an encircling
reflective pool.

Subtle shades of blue, green and grey soften the strong architectural features of the home.

Larger than life 3' x 3' concrete stepping stones serve as floating pads between the plantings and guide visitors from the driveway to the front door.

Strategically positioned lighting casts dramatic shadows and forms distinct outlines against the walls.

A composite wood walkway leads visitors through the Zen like xeriscape to the front door.

A Buddha head fountain at the front entrance can be viewed from the interior dining room.

Imported Mexican beach pebble adds a soft round palette for the sharp angular leaves of the Americana agave.

PROJECT KEY

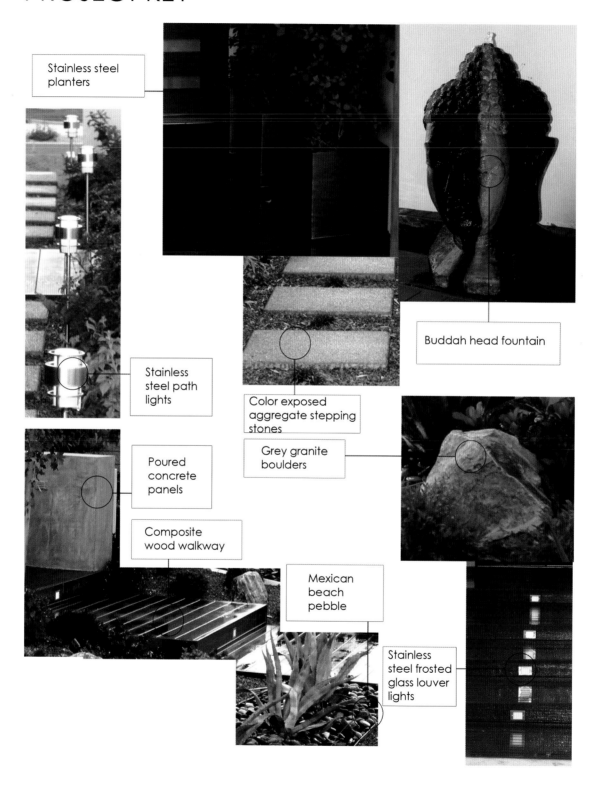

Stainless steel planters

Stainless steel path lights

Color exposed aggregate stepping stones

Buddah head fountain

Poured concrete panels

Grey granite boulders

Composite wood walkway

Mexican beach pebble

Stainless steel frosted glass louver lights

PLANT MATERIALS

1. Little Gem Magnolia
2. Bronze Loquat
3. Angelita Daisy
4. Eucalyptus Tree
5. Japanese Privet
6. Moonbay Nandina
7. Weeping Yucca
8. Agave Americana

Dining on the Edge

It's all about entertainment for a casino executive and his wife and their backyard says it all in true Las Vegas style. To accommodate a large dinner party, the outdoor kitchen was built as an extension to the one indoors. A buffet style countertop wraps completely around the area to the fireplace, like a warm embrace to keep the guests socializing. Beyond the fireplace, the natural slope of the property created the perfect backdrop for a cascading waterfall and stream system. Flagstone steps meander gently upward to a flagstone patio and seating area at the summit. The panoramic view of the Las Vegas valley makes the ascent more than worthwhile. Only a few steps away at the top of the berm, an outdoor billiard table rests on a level concrete slab awaiting challengers. At the base of the berm, a well groomed putting green with lush manicured fringe will test the skills of even a pro.

Artist conception of the design.

Photography by Eryn Ence.

The fireplace at the edge of the outdoor kitchen keeps guests warm and socializing.

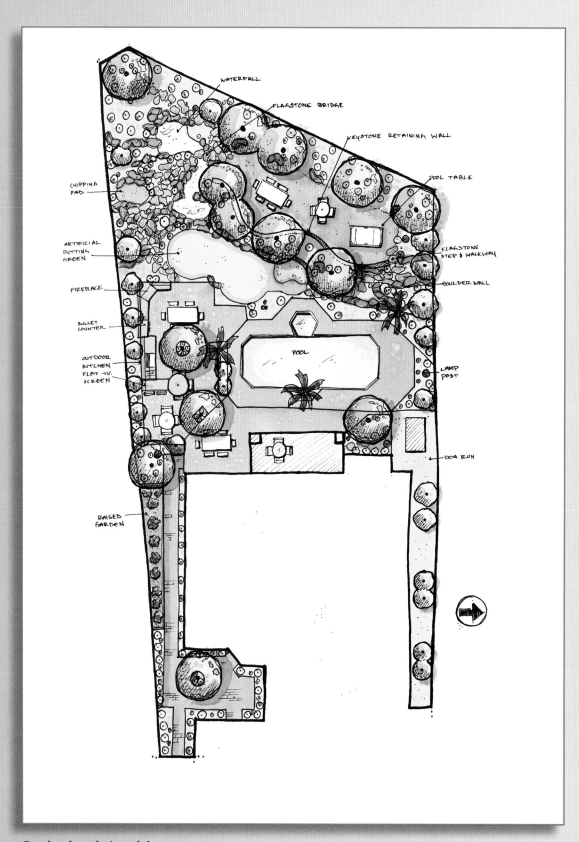

WATERFALL

FLAGSTONE BRIDGE

KEYSTONE RETAINING WALL

POOL TABLE

CHIPPING PAD

ARTIFICIAL PUTTING GREEN

FIREPLACE

BULLET COUNTER

OUTDOOR KITCHEN FLAT T.V. SCREEN

RAISED GARDEN

FLAGSTONE STEP & WALKWAY

BOULDER WALL

POOL

LAMP POST

DOG RUN

Overhead rendering of the property.

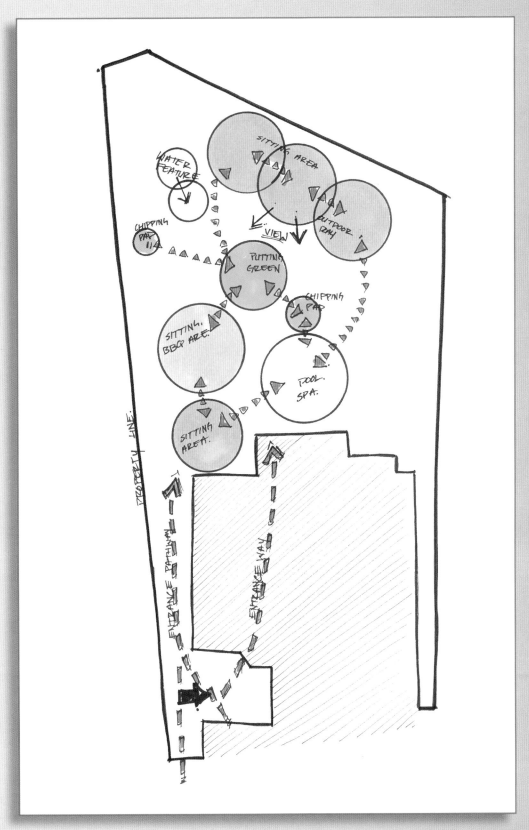

Concept plan.

Before images.

The eating countertop gives diners a view of the fireplace and waterfall while socializing with the cook.

An outdoor billiards table awaits challengers on top of the berm.

Naturally blending with the rocky desert outcroppings nearby, large boulders terrace the hillside and help level the putting green area.

The layout and design of the food preparation and dining area accommodate a large dinner party.

An herb garden located just steps from the outdoor kitchen serves as a fresh spice rack.

A pre-existing slope was transformed into a flowing stream and waterfall system.
Photography by Eryn Ence.

The lush fringe and manicured putting green of synthetic turf will impress even a pro.
Photography by Eryn Ence.

A rustic stacked stone fireplace blends seamlessly with the outdoor kitchen.
Photography by Eryn Ence.

Flagstone steps meander gently upward, bridging over the stream and beside the cascading water. Photography by Eryn Ence.

A buffet style countertop of sealed flagstone maintains the southwestern theme. Photography by Eryn Ence.

Anchoring the outdoor kitchen, the fireplace provides comfort and beauty. Photography by Eryn Ence.

An LCD outdoor television assures you can cook like a celebrity chef. Photography by Eryn Ence.

Viewed from above, it's easy to see how the dining area envelopes the visitor. Photography by Eryn Ence.

An elegant wrought iron fence keeps billiard players from stepping over the edge. Photography by Eryn Ence.

An illuminated green keeps the play going into the night.

The waterfall
generates
the soothing
sounds of
rushing
water.

Photography by Eryn Ence.

Photography by Eryn Ence.

The blazing fireplace warms even those seated at the eating countertop.

PROJECT KEY

Wrought iron fence

Stone veneer

Outdoor LCD flatscreen

Countertop BBQ light

Lynx ™ BBQ grill

Lynx ™ Cocktail Pro

Trash drawer

3-drawer storage

Refrigerator

2-drawer paper towel

Flagstone stack steps

Putting green

Iridescent glass path light

Waterfall

Keystone ™ wall

Apache brown boulder

PLANT MATERIALS

1. Magnolia
2. Purple Lantana
3. Purple Leaf Plum
4. Dwarf Japanese Garden Jupiter
5. Radiation Lantana
6. Vegetable Garden
7. Peach Tree
8. Red Carpet Rose

Inspire to Retire

Spending the golden years of retirement overlooking the rolling hills of a pristine golf course would fulfill the dream of most couples. But these homeowners wanted to complete their landscape with personal touches that have brought them joy throughout their lives. The residents have called the Southwest home for many years and have grown to love its rugged beauty and rustic charm. Low maintenance xeriscape was a must for the property.

Dear to their hearts from a trip abroad, a water feature is perfectly replicated in the courtyard, the soothing sounds of rushing water echoing within its confines. Year round reminiscing is assured by a warming firepit and comfortable seating. Adjacent to the back of the house, the outdoor kitchen takes full advantage of the brilliant sunsets over Red Rock Canyon, west of the Las Vegas valley.

Artist conception of the design.

Photography by Carl Pantuso.

Inspired by a trip abroad, a natural stone water feature was replicated from a photograph.

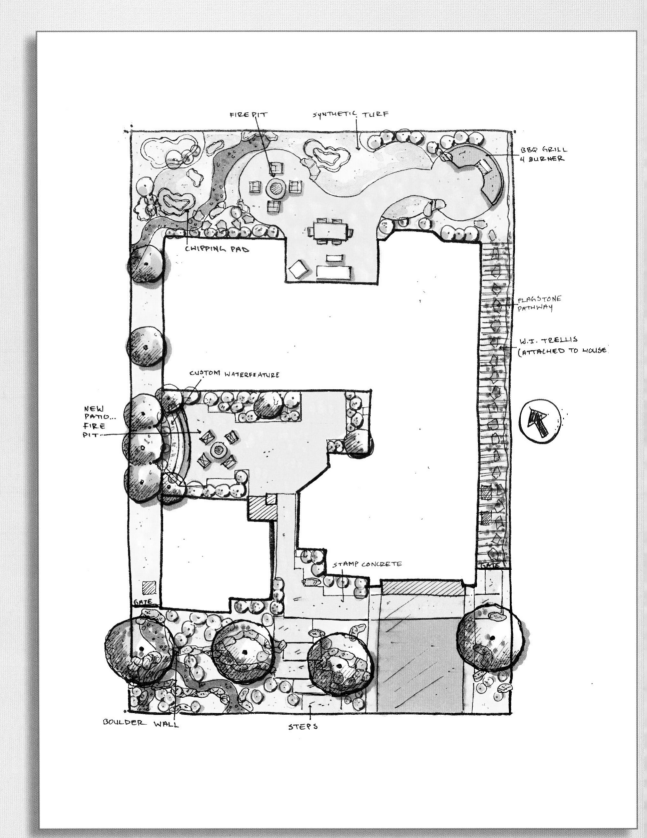

FIRE PIT   SYNTHETIC TURF

BBQ GRILL
4 BURNER

CHIPPING PAD

FLAGSTONE
PATHWAY

W.I. TRELLIS
(ATTACHED TO HOUSE)

CUSTOM WATERFEATURE

NEW
PATIO...
FIRE
PIT...

GATE

STAMP CONCRETE

GATE

BOULDER WALL   STEPS

Overhead rendering of the property.

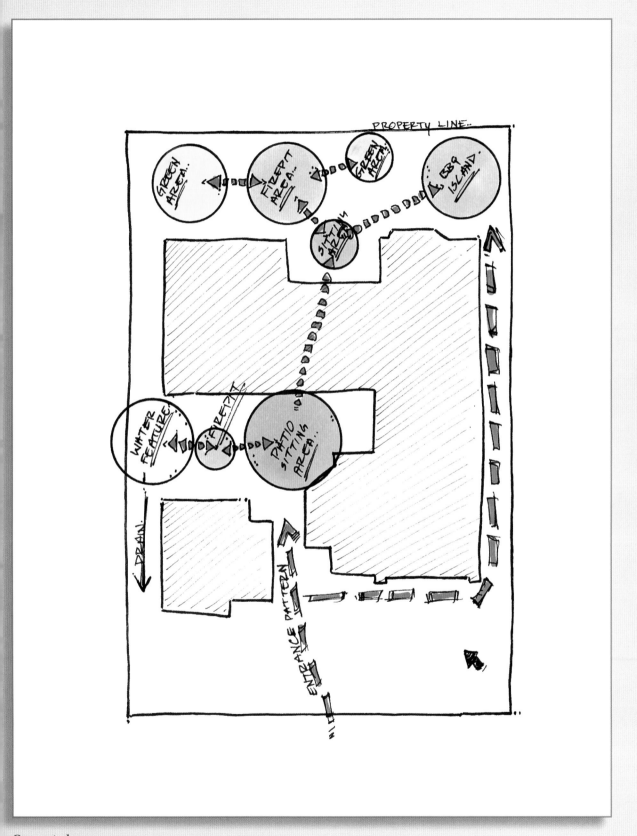

Concept plan.

Before images.

Golden hues on the rock material in three varying sizes offset the vegetation and add texture. Photography by Carl Pantuso.

The desert look is so authentic; the front yard seems to have been transplanted from just outside the city limits.

The natural design
in the front yard
included native plants
and a dry creek bed.
Photography by Carl
Pantuso.

The soothing sounds of over flowing water echo in the confines of the courtyard. Photography by Carl Pantuso.

A touch of rustic western charm was added to the barbecue and firepit with matching natural flagstone. Photography by Carl Pantuso.

The dry creek bed begins at the back of the property and continues to the front. Photography by Carl Pantuso.

Synthetic turf ties the yard to the golf course beyond.
Photography by Carl Pantuso.

Photography by Carl Pantuso.

A custom arbor supports a natural canopy of fragrant star jasmine.
Photography by Carl Pantuso.

The outdoor
kitchen overlooks
the rolling hills
of a pristine golf
course.

A dramatic fire
and water effect
pleasantly surprises
guests arriving at the
front door.

Photography by Carl Pantuso.

A warming firepit installed in front of the water feature ensures enjoyment year round. Photography by Carl Pantuso.

A firepit provides warmth while watching the sunset behind the Red Rock Canyon west of the Las Vegas valley.
Photography by Carl Pantuso.

PROJECT KEY

Synthetic turf

Side burner/
storage drawer

4-burner
BBQ grill

Custom trellis
archway

Stamped
concrete

Gold granite
boulder

Quartzite
flagstone

1'' thick quartzite
flagstone

Sheer descent

Quartzite
flagstone pathway

Lava rock

Quartzite
flagstone
cap

PLANT MATERIALS

1. Red fountain Grass
2. French Lavender
3. Kangaroo Paw
4. New Gold Lantana
5. Golden Barrel
6. Ocotillo

Sensory Conception

Like the pioneers before them, these homeowners migrated to escape the long harsh winters of the east. The search for mild seasons brought them to the Southwest, but the rugged beauty, bright clear colors and bold contrasts made them stay. Adopting the southwestern lifestyle, they created the perfect environment for social gathering and gracious hospitality.

Throughout the yard is a cross pollination of styles, materials and textures paying tribute to the diverse cultural influence that shaped the territory. The striking contrasts add complexity and depth while awakening the senses of sight, sound, smell and touch. The sense of taste is found at the outdoor kitchen, of course.

Artist conception of the design.

The sharp spines of a steel yucca mimic those of a natural Americana agave.

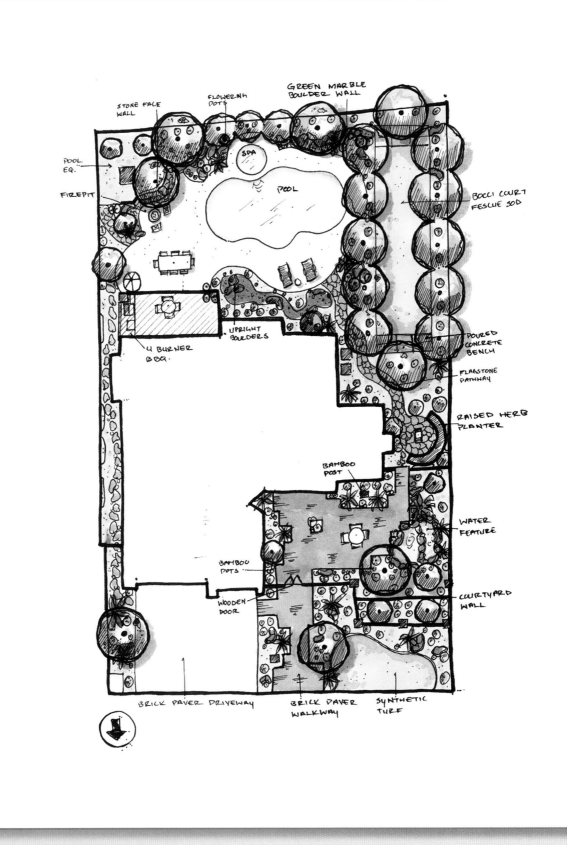

STONE FACE WALL

FLOWERING POTS

GREEN MARBLE BOULDER WALL

POOL EQ.

FIREPIT

SPA

POOL

BOCCI COURT FESCUE SOD

4 BURNER BBQ.

UPRIGHT BOULDERS

POURED CONCRETE BENCH

FLAGSTONE PATHWAY

RAISED HERB PLANTER

BAMBOO POST

WATER FEATURE

BAMBOO POTS

COURTYARD WALL

WOODEN DOOR

BRICK PAVER DRIVEWAY

BRICK PAVER WALKWAY

SYNTHETIC TURF

Overhead rendering of the property.

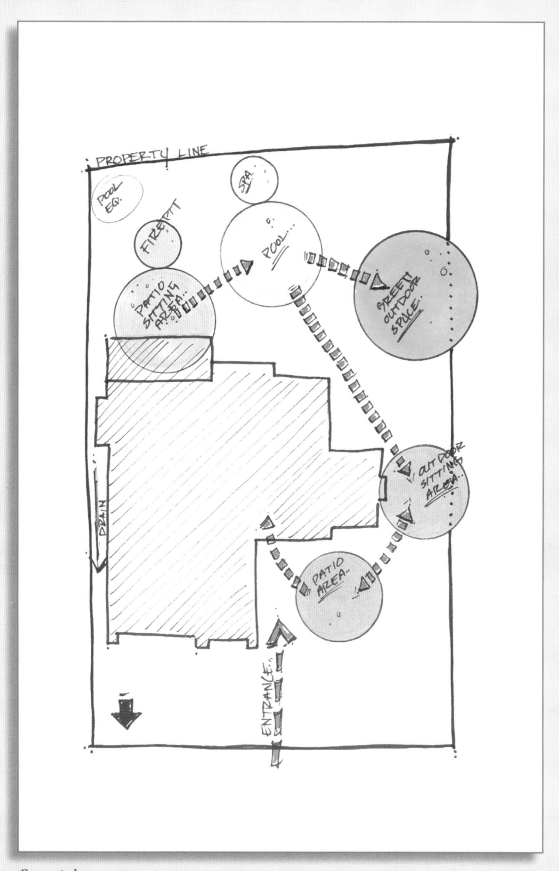

Concept plan.

Before images.

A bang metal pot balances the height of the Ocotillo against the house.

Erect grey granite boulders resembling Stonehenge complete a Zen like rock garden.

A curved stone
veneer wall
provides seating
for the firepit while
cleverly masking
the unsightly pool
equipment.

Metal stars
and rustic
flowers are
scattered
around to
add a touch
of whimsy.

Like the
varied
cultures
that shaped
the region,
the yard
is a cross
pollination
of designs,
styles and
materials.

Green granite juts out to mimic the jagged mountains nearby.

Spectacular flowers bloom from cactus.

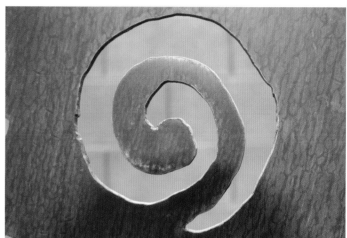

Culturally diverse garden art adds interest to the yard.

The vibrant colored blossoms climbing the columns match the bang metal pots at the base.

The curved shape of the pool and spa mask the straight line of the property wall.

Soft rounded corners are accented with iridescent mosaic glass tile which shimmers in the light and changes hues as the sun sets.

Rustic flagstone was used for the countertop and shelving.

The refreshment center is perfect for entertaining.

The contrast
in textures and
materials lend
complexity, scale
and depth to the
area.

Shoestring acacia shade the bocce ball court.

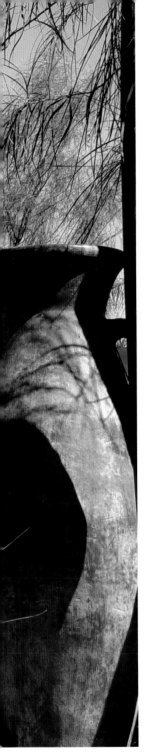

Left:
Pots filled with annual flowers burst color year round.

A metal sunflower opens to reveal live plants at the center.

The firepit beckons family and friends to gather around and recount stories of the past.

The dining table is within arm's reach of the outdoor kitchen.

The enclosed outer room is visible from the bocce ball court.

Urns and spill pots add character throughout the yard.

Outdoor
lighting
enables
socializing
into the late
night hours.

A gentle stream of water spills into the pool.

A comfortable couch entices visitors to spend time outdoors.

PROJECT KEY

Paper towel dispenser

River rock

Gray granite bouder

Oceanside ™ glass tile

Lynz ™ 52''Pro-Sear grill

Refrigerator

Cocktail Pro Lynx ™

Utensil holder

Bottle holder

Bocci ball court

Bocci ball bench

Bang metal pot

Spiral stair case

Mexican pot

Green granite

Veneer stone firepit

Pool equipment behind wall

PLANT MATERIALS

1. Red Yucca
2. Dwarf Bottlebrush
3. New Gold Lantana
4. Agave Americana
5. Vinca
6. Gazania
7. Foxtail Fern
8. Sago Palm
9. Japanese Blueberry

Three-part Harmony

The goal for this project was to create perfect harmony in a backyard landscape dominated by a pre-existing pool. The homeowners, a dancer and jazz singer, wanted to be able to entertain…naturally. A cleverly designed outdoor kitchen and dining area was situated into the small space between the house and the pool, alleviating trips inside the home and accidental falls into the water. While a fireplace keeps dishes warm as the main course is prepared, a lattice awning above assures the guests are cool and comfortable dining *alfresco*. Lacking in greenery, a *trompe l'oeil* mural was painted on the perimeter wall, brought to life with natural plant material spread throughout the area. Key to cooling off in style is a refreshing dip in the pool and a sip of a drink at the swim-up bar.

Artist conception of the design.

The backyard
arrangement
sets the perfect
tone for dining,
entertaining and
relaxing.

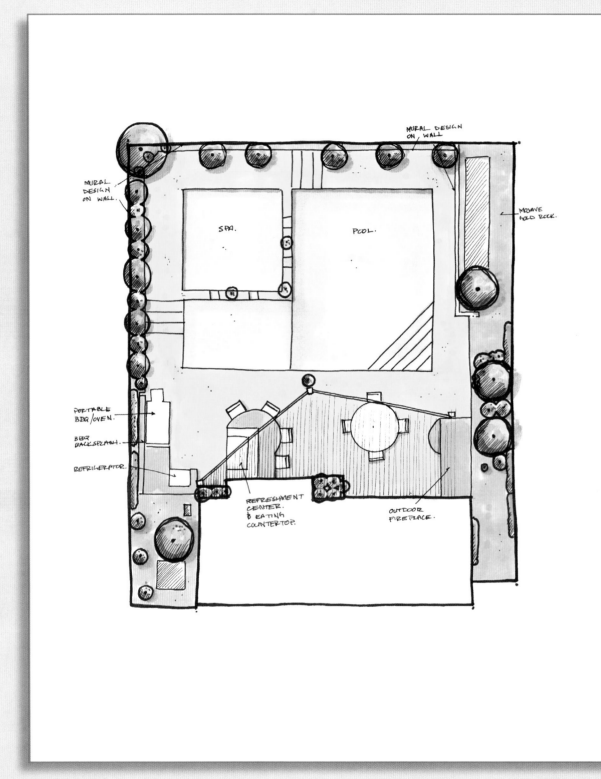

Overhead rendering of the property.

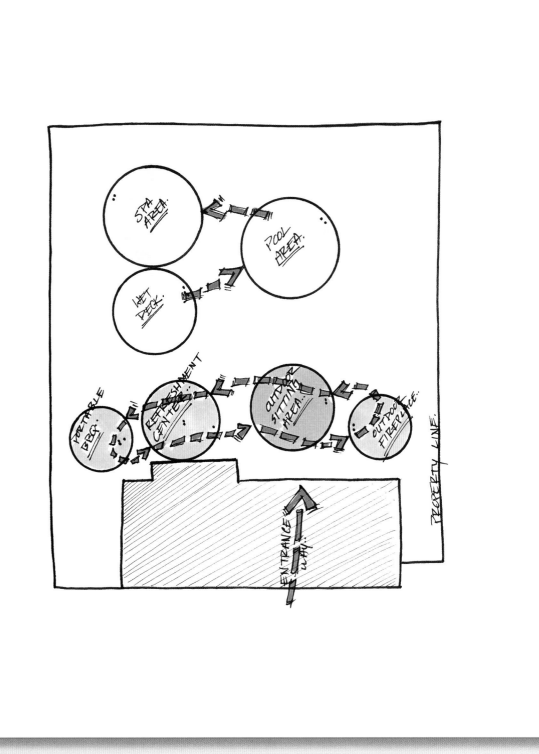

Concept plan.

Before images.

Climbing bougainvillea and wisteria add vibrant color and sweet fragrance to the area.

Natural
flagstone caps
the storage
nook, mantle,
pot shelf and
hearth of the
fireplace.

Live trees, shrubs and flowers almost make the property wall disappear.

Ornamental trees are a source of privacy for the spa.

A trompe l'oeil mural painted on the wall adds greenery and interest, but natural plant material makes it come to life.

The outdoor bar and sitting area keeps everyone socializing.

Contained in decorative pots, the fruit and citrus trees blend seamlessly with the wall.

A swim up bar
is guaranteed
to refresh.

Mounted on
the wall is a
musical staff
complete with
notes and a
treble cleff.

The refreshment center easily serves those seated at the
bar height countertop.

The faux finish
paint on the
fireplace face
gives a suede like
appearance.

A corridor
kitchen fits
in the small
space, yet still
allows the cook
preparation
area.

With a large grill and outdoor oven you can cater a large dinner party.

PROJECT KEY

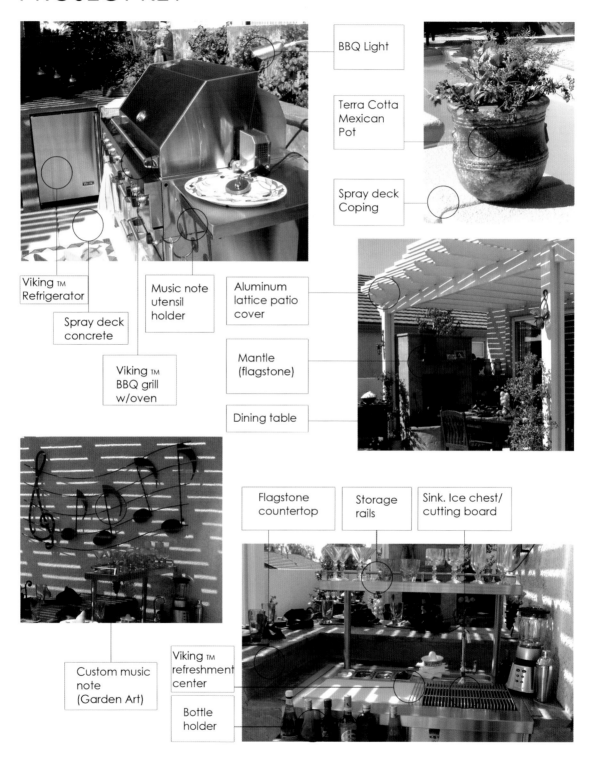

BBQ Light

Terra Cotta Mexican Pot

Spray deck Coping

Viking ™ Refrigerator

Spray deck concrete

Music note utensil holder

Viking ™ BBQ grill w/oven

Aluminum lattice patio cover

Mantle (flagstone)

Dining table

Flagstone countertop

Storage rails

Sink. Ice chest/ cutting board

Custom music note (Garden Art)

Viking ™ refreshment center

Bottle holder

PLANT MATERIALS

1. Bottle Tree
2. Pin Cushion Flower
3. Bouganvilla Vine
4. Lemon Tree Meyer
5. Carolina Cherry Laurel